Love Letters
&
Pocket Knives

poems

J.J. Celli

central
avenue

2025

"I Cannot Throw Love Out The Window" was first published in *The Central Avenue
Poetry Prize 2024*, Central Avenue Publishing, 2024.

Published by Central Avenue Poetry, an imprint of Central Avenue Marketing Ltd.
www.centralavenuepublishing.com

LOVE LETTERS AND POCKET KNIVES

Trade Paperback: 978-1-77168-401-9
Epub: 978-1-77168-402-6

Published in Canada
Printed in United States of America

1. POETRY / LGBTQ+ 2. POETRY / Women Authors

1 3 5 7 9 10 8 6 4 2

Contents

Part I - Brass Knuckle

Regret — 3

Does It Hurt? — 4

Poem to Earlier Self — 5

Keeping — 6

As Long as Time Permits — 7

Gone Mad — 8

The Thunder Took Rest to the Shotgun Sounds Between Us — 9

Have Been — 10

Closer Look — 13

Too Far Gone — 14

Exhale — 15

In the Shadows of Us — 16

Linger — 17

Feeling You Up — 18

Through My Walls, Whisper — 19

Sound of a Ticking Turn Signal — 20

Sense of Longing — 21

Angel — 22

On Getting Over — 23

Part II - Switchblade

Closed Fist — 27

Tossed — 28

All Streets — 29

Where I Learned Not to Sleep — 30

What Keeps — 31

The Crest of the Ilium — 32

How We Burn — 33

Within You — 34

Before You Leave — 35

Don't Speak — 36

Neurotic — 37

Thinking You Here — 40

Asked Not to Know — 41

Teenage Tenderness — 42

Something Else Breathing — 45

When Words Fall Away — 46

Eighth Note Groove — 47

Good Intentions — 48

Be Her(e) Again — 49

Who We Wish We Were — 50

They Say It Takes Thirty Days to Make or Break a Habit — 51

Part III - Swiss Army

Breaking Night (Urban Slang to Mean Staying Up Until Morning) — 55

What's Broken — 56

Crushed Cardboard Container — 57

If You See Her — 58

Last Night Again — 60

Bitter Farewell — 61

Should Have Checked Caller ID — 65

Perception — 66

Antithetical — 67

In Greek Mythology, Echo Is a Nymph Who Proclaimed Her Love of Narcissus Until Nothing Was Left of Her but Her Voice — 68

Black Crow & Gravel Roads — 70

We Sang Along in Rebellion and Made Out in the Name of Self-Expression — 71

Reflection — 73

Burning Bridges, Burning Sage — 74

Gone Now — 76

Ghost — 78

Part IV - Butterfly

January Twenty-Ninth — 81

Admit, We Could Go On Like This Forever — 82

In the Rain — 83

Warmer Seasons — 84

Hope — 85

I Cannot Throw Love Out the Window — 86

Lessons from the Weather — 87

Porch Lights — 88

The Poem That Finds You in the Middle of Moving On — 89

Happiness Is — 90

Forty-Two Miles Away — 92

Actually, a Love Poem — 93

What to Say to the They Sitting on the Curb in Front of Barnes and Noble — 95

The Feelings Between Us Changed Color — 97

Bird Hours — 98

Is-ness of Things — 99

Blackberry Brandy — 101

Forward My Mail to Mars — 102

And Not Look Back — 103

Pocket Knives — 105

Wild Words — 106

On Writers — 107

Dear Reader,

Pocket knives have always fascinated me—the sharp edge, the quiet promise of protection. I carry one always, a constant companion. In staying true to this part of myself, I've chosen four of my favorite blades to represent distinct phases of this poetic journey. As you travel with me through *Love Letters & Pocket Knives,* you'll find the path is neither gentle nor smooth. We will move through many loves and lovers, each moment and memory cutting its unique shape into who I am.

Part I—Brass Knuckle. Where we begin. It's fierce, passionate, sometimes violent—just like the first rush of love, where power meets vulnerability. A brass knuckle knife feels like armor but is dangerous when used carelessly. In the thrill of connection, we can be reckless, even destructive. A blade leaves an imprint of intensity like a bruise, a moment of impact that lingers beneath the surface, unseen but present, as we slowly heal.

Part II—Switchblade. These poems capture moments that cut deep like a thin blade that is precise, intense, and mysterious, often hidden until it's too late. You'll find betrayal and seduction balanced against adoration and intimacy. The switchblade represents the sharpness of words, the silent breaks, and the delicate edge that divides love from letting go.

Part III—Swiss Army. This blade is versatile, much like the stages of healing and growth. It holds within it a complexity of emotions, a readiness to confront the challenges of life and love. The Swiss Army knife symbolizes the adaptability we cultivate as we move forward, equipped with the tools we need to navigate our ever-evolving journey.

Part IV—Butterfly. Unlike the others, it flows with grace and fluidity—a symbol of transformation. This blade reflects both skill and poise. In practiced hands, it moves elegantly, embodying mastery. The butterfly knife is metamorphosis, the shedding of the past, and the emergence of something stronger, more resilient, and more beautiful for the difficulties we've survived.

Yours,
JJ

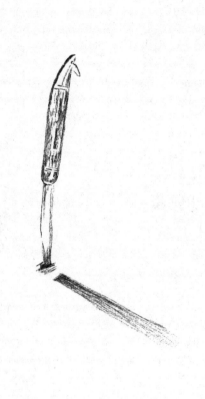

Love Letters & Pocket Knives

PART I
BRASS KNUCKLE

Not even poetry is always strong—
every line must eventually break.

REGRET

I will not regret the end.
The crash, burn, and destruction.
The discontent, silence, and regret.
The rage.

When we don't want or care
to know each other any longer.
When love goes lost but we can't let go.

Still, I am not afraid of giving every
last piece of everything I am.

No, I will not regret the way we end.

I will regret surviving.

DOES IT HURT?

I am often asked what it felt like and whether it hurt, but I hardly remember the feeling. Having a searing hot one-inch piece of metal traveling through your body at approximately 1,200 miles per hour does not hurt (at first). The lead core encased in harder copper from a full metal jacket stays intact, designed to penetrate skin tissue with as little damage as possible. A cleaner but deeper wound channel. Less fatal. I am lucky she chose the ammo carelessly, not using hollow point, a round that expands like a mushroom as it travels, a design created to cause more immediate, dramatic, and severe damage.

Being shot is a sudden, jolting impact followed by no sensation. Nothing. The feeling at first is in the mind: ringing, clinging, deafening, like oversized wind chimes banging violently against one another, but worse. A numbing noise I will never forget, I cannot forget. The real pain comes afterward—hours, weeks, months. Years still. An extreme burning, veins a circuit fire, body full of electricity, flames igniting right below the skin and racing and roaring rapidly up and down the arm. There is little to do but let it burn, let neuropathy take what it will.

Chronic pain follows throughout recovery—and you never fully recover. You just get better at managing and ignoring the hurt response, pushing and dragging the breaking point of tolerance, and of course the psychological trauma. The talk of a *love like ours* taunts like a dirty joke or something funny, or both. Maybe that's it; that's what it feels like to have been shot. Sure, my physical body was strong enough to survive, but it's about all the parts inside afterward that died. That's the part that hurts.

POEM TO EARLIER SELF

How dare you sit there,
knees tucked into your chest, doing nothing,
like some weak child.
       Who taught you that?
I don't care if you were shot!
You know better than to wear your pain
like an advertisement across the front of that blood-soiled T-shirt;
       I did not teach you that!

You have legs, fists, a voice.
You could use them.
Instead, you do nothing
but bleed out onto the floor.
       Damn you!
Much of our blood now lost.

If that were me, I'd have said exactly what I thought.
Would have uncurled our damaged body,
bled all over her,
cast the mangled, hanging skin from our arm out
onto the walls
like red Rorschach inkblots
spattered across the vaulted ceiling, said,
       See this? See this?

Held the inside of our wound
as close to her face as possible,
making sure she never forgot the smell of real blood,
that copper-penny scent, our raw meat.

A decade ago, we were not the same.
I was *you,* but *you*—
No. *You* were not me.

KEEPING

Even our secrets keep secrets.

AS LONG AS TIME PERMITS

You broke into my imagination,
turned my eyes off, sex on.
I won't shame you
for not wanting something beautiful.
For not asking for something real.

In simply wanting to
slam our bodies together
and just be.

GONE MAD

So tell me, where does the heart go when love goes mad and turns crazy? When love goes out on the weekends and no longer wants to come home. When love won't take your calls or call back even after the thirteenth time you've dialed. When the back door, always left open in case one of us gets locked out, gets locked. No spare key under the doormat or in the potted plants.

Tell me where the heart goes when the dog still needs to be walked and the yard mowed before the leaves start to fall faster and quicker than we can keep up. Winter is long enough in the Midwest without adding a cold shoulder and cold eyes to things that don't need help freezing over.

The heart can't just stop feeling, like hands can, or the mind when it turns bitter. Not like the moon can when she is forced to spend her nights half in her own shadow, staring at all those stars, pretty and bright. Watching as they fall, dance, and chase each other across the sky, all flirty and in love, all the damn time. Even when alone, the stars can still turn themselves on—

But tell me, where does the heart go?

THE THUNDER TOOK REST TO THE SHOTGUN SOUNDS BETWEEN US

The rain and I kept driving.
Next to me, my lover cried.
In front of me, the windshield cried.

Between her screams, the violent thunder, and these wipers
was the saddest song
I think the rain and I
had ever heard.

HAVE BEEN

I

I have been one too many shots on a Tuesday at 3 p.m.,
or a Thursday.
Been one Violent Femmes song,
one glass of red wine, away from
a quick fix to bring on
those nights that started at noon and made blackouts feel safe.
Being passed out was safer than who I was awake.

Cutting Adderall, Modafinil, and when I didn't want to feel at all,
there was Vicodin and Dilaudid to help me forget the things I did.

I still haven't been sober as many years as I spent drunk,
not realizing it was a good thing when you asked for nothing more than
the sober me,
the honest me.
The me I had no idea how to be,
as I had never been that person before. I have been many lies told to
honest souls
for fun and revenge,
for wanting to take you home
just to see if I could.

I have been many secrets
whispered by straight girls that *this doesn't count*,
it's just a wanting, a trying,
to see what it's like to kiss a girl.

I have been touching my thoughts inappropriately, your thoughts
inappropriately,
this single-minded affair
over time, or was it time after time?

I have been sweet-talker and love letters,
been pocket knives in bar fights,
been jumped in parking lots by dyke-fearing, homophobic tough guys.
Been broken nose, broken bones,
been two black eyes.

I have been careless, negligent,
guard down. Been victim
under gunpoint, under fire,
shot by my furious ex-lover,
those hands touched and loved under
now used violently to harm me.

Been another bad choice,
fucked up emotionally and physically
by someone who said they cared for me.

I have been worn out, strung out,
been one last drink driving home,
driving off the road,
thoughts of suicide.

I have been half alive,
pissing in the shower while shaving my head,
screaming, crying, bleeding.
Been better off dead.

I have been almost ready, almost better,
almost sober.

I have been one too many excuses from facing myself,
one too many goddamn times.

II

I am not that now.

III

I am now
Sunday's rest in a weekday body,
early morning coffee and a trusting somebody.
I am open.
No more pathetic lies.
I am honest with my heart and faithful between my thighs.

And I am sorry I couldn't have been this then; I just wasn't ready.

I am falling in love in late September
over and over again.
I am faithful, full of transparency,
her never needing to question my loyalty.

I am slowly making this *I Am*
the person you remember.

I am not the past.
I am not who I have been.
I am right now.
I am now.
I Am.

CLOSER LOOK

I search
inside of you
(those eyes, mouth, hands, touch, the softest and hardest parts of your
heart)
for feelings, for love
that will not hurt.

TOO FAR GONE

and out of my mind,
far ahead of my body,
stuck inside those places of my past again.

Can you feel me reach for you?
Placing your palm gently against my breastbone,
asking you to pull me back
into this human night.

EXHALE

In the furthest bedroom
I light a candle.
Standing in front of the open window,
I take a hit,
the pocket-sized wooden pipe
still packed with remnants of a stale green plant material.

I feel fifteen again,
like I am still hiding
from parents and streetlights,
squad cars and adolescence.

Those years that asked
for nothing less than everything.

IN THE SHADOWS OF US

She meets me in one of those nameless night places
where the dark is a street sign, empty parking lot, vacant house on
Second Street.
The dark is the back seat of her car.
My clothes.
Two bodies.
Where I cover her mouth with my mouth,
fill my body with her body
as if she can make me something holy.
Here, alone in dark places
where we can't see
who we've become.

LINGER

Remind me how a kiss begs to linger, to carry a wanting that doesn't leave just because we ask it to. How a kiss loiters, walks a thin line between being passionate and being obsessive. How it waits outside the body, looking for any opportunity to jump its way back into our mouths. How many different places a kiss can touch, and keep, besides our lips. How a kiss becomes consequential, transformational, taking us places we do not *ever* come back from. Breaking us in ways from which we never fully recover.

FEELING YOU UP

There's still this photograph, us
lying in a dandelion summer,
faces shaded by the weeping willow tree
seconds before I slip my hand up your shirt,
when I still believe we can touch each other
and not change.

THROUGH MY WALLS, WHISPER

Push your hands against my doors,
your ear to my music,
your mouth to my window,
your back against my stone.

Your eyes, *yes*, your eyes
to my closed riverbeds,
my cloudy still-water silhouette.

Throw your pebbles against my shadow,
your yellow wings, red horns,
your feelings to my falling.

Gather me. Slip into me.
A little slower, *yes*,
come a little closer.

SOUND OF A TICKING TURN SIGNAL

I needed to rest it.
Resist the urge to window shop,
even in the clouds.
See, touch, and hold what I couldn't have.
Pocket-and-dip, hit-and-ditch.
Sure, it was something,
but feeding a lion a canary
still wouldn't be enough.

That brings me here.
Among a stationary "us,"
tired and sad, sitting
surveying traffic lights.
A slow change from yellow to red to green.

After waiting in line for miles,
only a few kilometers traveled.
And the turn signal shouts
through the silence of my truck:

don't go–don't go–don't go–don't go

SENSE OF LONGING

I am not the only one done and undone by my madness,
by simple, non-moving things
as in a name, yours—
the whole world in the letters of it,
the sound it carries as it travels
the channels of my eardrum.
　The sound of your sigh, your low hum
lingers,
a blindfold over my eyes.
Cover me, shake me,
rattle out the way these years
have had their way with me.
Underneath,
I'm wanting,
waiting
to wear you
again.

ANGEL

You never asked me to come for you,
didn't light incense or send smoke signals to the gods,
didn't cast out messages in bottles, make ritual chants,
singing like perched songbirds of summer.

Between these days dragging,
drag queens,
>   *their green eye shadow, glitter, Pals Breast Forms, beautifully and*
>   *flamboyantly flaunting femininity*
drag shows,
>   *another glamorous lip-syncing performance*
and drags off your Marlboro Red,
the halos in smoke rings,
innocence in secondhand smoke
and sex in shotguns,
I waited.

Did you think I wouldn't wait?
That my body wouldn't wait for you?

How you come. Sin inside me.
Between your classic skin-colored pantyhose over your see-through
white lace thong,
that lipstick in lethal red you smear for your Sunday love affair with the
Lord.

It's only in dreams we go to heaven.

Standing in line with all those pale-colored saints
calling you *Angel*?

God dammit!
I always called you
Angel.

ON GETTING OVER

Maybe I need to rent a room in some cheap motel, the kind you can pay for by the hour. A room with no working shower or hot running water, no telephone, just a coverless, sticky phone book dated like 1979. A room with one nightstand, broken top drawer, cracked mirror, and no cable. A place that doesn't even have a paved parking lot and comes with a lengthy list of janitorial and mechanical problems—broken bulbs on the corner sign too old to even glow. The type of place with vintage coral pink lawn chairs missing most seat straps. Set up in parking spots as if there is any view around except the vending machine that sells pop, Doritos, condoms, and tampons, all for a buck.

Someplace off a two-lane road next to a cornfield and a Casey's, White Castle, or a Jack in the Box. Places that aren't made for healthy living. The type of room where you go to fuck or kill yourself, just four dirty walls that beg and foam at the mouth for sex or suicide. Or maybe you're willing to entertain both, just to feel yourself feeling something again. Right now, I am not looking to do either one, but I know it is going to take some extreme measure, waking up in someplace sadder, sicker, and lonelier than I am to wake up, at least once, not thinking about you.

PART II
SWITCHBLADE

Lead me with breadcrumbs, not a leash.

CLOSED FIST

I have broken more promises than bones,
more hearts than bad habits,
am more broken windows
than opened doors,
more dead ends than open roads.

More cemetery than church,
more county morgue than waiting room,
where good news is *not* delivered,
not those tears of happiness that fill the floors
for every good reason,
like someone healed, recovered,
or simply survived.

I am easy to love,
hard to hold,
too sharp, too split, too severed at the edges,
too much closed fist.
Graffiti. Litter.
Dangerous.

I have lied when I should have been truthful,
said *yes* when I meant *no*,
said *no* when it was in my best interest to say *yes*.

Haven't said *please*, *sorry*, or *forgive me*
nearly enough,
and I've rarely said *love* when inside
I know I meant it.

TOSSED

Your smile lets me down easy; it's those eyes
that throw me to the ground.

ALL STREETS

She said she liked the way I walked:
broad shoulders, far bigger than I was.
How I spit on sidewalks,
took up more space than I needed.

How I kissed her in public the same way I did in private.
The way I said *fuck* and it never sounded wrong.
How she just couldn't walk around saying things
all abrasive and vulgar like that.

She said I looked and sounded the same. If she could only
figure out how to describe what that was.

Like I was *all streets* or something.

Said I stood like I was always protecting:
the checkout line at the grocery store, the gas pump,
the doorway as she dressed and undressed.

I think she just liked girls who took refuge in their boyhood.
Girls in leather boots, ripped-up blue jeans, baggy sweatshirts, and
boxer briefs.

Girls that were mistaken in public restrooms.
Girls that intimidated people, even though they never tried.

I think she just liked girls who were somewhere between reckless and wild,
somewhere between hers and theirs.
As long as they were hers most of the time.

She said girls like that loved deeper and appreciated being nurtured. I
guess that was right.
I mean, I rarely admitted it, but she was the one doing the hard work,
taking care of me.

Even though I was the one who she said walked around all boss,
all tough, *all streets*.

WHERE I LEARNED NOT TO SLEEP

I usually leave it cracked open, ya know,
that door, my mouth,
when both should be
pulled and pressed tight,
slammed shut.
I continue to welcome the cool draft, the white noise,
the charred grit of a tooth grind,
the hesitation before I hurt myself
again.
Slightly ajar
past the six panels arranged in two vertical columns,
recessed wood of texture and depth
like the good genes of a strong jawline.
Both stern and solid.
Behind the door, I am the temperature of the sun,
a burnt-out star,
flame over spoon,
leather gloves,
a bit of heat
keeping your thighs and your hands warm.

A lover in our bed,
in your mind,
in your throat
when you push in
what you can't take back.

Sweet and thick,
a tablespoon of farmers' market
organic honey.
Swallow—it helps the medicine go,
helps to force it *all*
back down.

WHAT KEEPS

It is your scars I can't see,
I feel the most.

THE CREST OF THE ILIUM

I watch you tread through shallow water,
parting the waves like the hips,
wide and familiar,
of that woman
we both know you still love.

HOW WE BURN

Looked at me like *Yes*,
said *Now*, said *Come*
down low enough as not to see a thing.

Until closed eyes
were the sun,
the night,
the day after tomorrow.

Looked at me like
you might believe I hadn't done this before.
Said *I can't teach you how to tame a lover*
from here though you're doing it right.

Until soft skin was pressed so close
it was impossible to be anything soft at all.

To know, now, is to know
the way we move in the dark.
The way we are the dark.
Covered in the delicate, secret spaces of each other.
We reach for, touch, each other's heat.
To see if together
we are still capable
of fire.

WITHIN YOU

I know I am not always
on your mind—
but you must feel me
inside you,
sleeping beside your soul.

BEFORE YOU LEAVE

Fill this bedroom
with eyes like romance
in love-soaked walls,
a color dark, of heavy wanting,
a scent of sweet patchouli
to linger and press against me
when you are no longer here.

DON'T SPEAK

Just take me
so I can hear you
in the air,
in the walls,
in the sheets.
In the things that hide and hold your warm body
in the dark on all these nights
when I am just a voice
on the other end of a tired phone.

NEUROTIC

My ex can tell you I'm a neurotic lover,
slightly jealous, borderline obsessive,
sometimes acting or going crazy,
or just fucking lonely.

How our bedtime conversations began to feel like criminal
interrogations
infusing good-cop-bad-cop tactics, psychological ploys to extract
information,
resulting in coerced, false confessions, or worse, truth,
the most valuable piece of incriminating evidence there is.

They can tell you I played the same sad songs over and over again,
blaming Michael Bolton for my breakdowns
as we took turns holding each other, lashing out, blaming the other.

They can tell you I was hurt and madness,
with issues of abandonment,
instability and promiscuity. That most of the time, I was out of my
goddamn mind.

Insomnia and dependency.
Dependent on just about everything.

They can tell you I'm sex shops, erotic entertainment,
leather covered with various harnesses.
Tell you I'm diner dives,
disreputable places, unglamorous,
with dim lighting and weak menus.

That I am spur-of-the-moment tattoos
just to feel a little pain or feel *something*.
How I was inside the law, but outside the thin blue line.

They can tell you I had gender dysphoria paired with rage,
up to almost two packs of Camel Wides a day.
All the painkillers
in orange-labeled containers.

Therapy on Wednesdays.

They can tell you I'm strong on the outside,
body of muscle and ink, obsessed with protein grams and calorie
intake.
(How contradicting, these judgments we make.)

Inside, I am fragile too.
I hope they also tell you that truth.
How I did my best to open myself up.

Disciplined to the point of fault.
Fearless and lovingly protective.
That when I said I'd do something, it got done with extreme care and
conviction.

I hope they tell you I am to-do lists, organized,
take pride in being the one that provides
financially, emotionally, and physically.

I hope they tell you I am grocery shopping on Sundays at noon,
dinner at six, dedicated to the commitment
of family and future first.

That I held their hand in public places, not shy or embarrassed
to press our bodies in passion
against mirrors in mall dressing rooms, theatres,
daylight, in the woods, back seat of their car.

My fingers hanging out of their back pocket, loose around the belt loop,
always showing, without saying, how I was proud to be next to them.

I hope they tell you how I held them as we slept,
one arm around the waist, the other cupping their breast.
Holding myself tight, as long as I could, to every
touchable part.

THINKING YOU HERE

An image from
somewhere I've never been.
You with them.
People I don't know,
don't want to know.

Your eyes confront me, I steal your smile.
Pocket and place it
here, and there, and here.

ASKED NOT TO KNOW

I know you dreamed of her again last night.
I felt her
when you held me.

TEENAGE TENDERNESS

Sitting cross-legged in a circle on the blue carpet in your bedroom,
listening to Skid Row in the dark. Your mom, high, just a room over
as we make up our own meaning of "18 and Life."
Passing around the Mad Dog and exchanging smiles and soft
hand touches when sharing the bottle. Silent invitations, wordless
reservations of who was with whom tonight.

In combat boots and flannels, all looking the same gender,
smoking Camel Wides and Cloves. Long bleached and purple bangs,
nose piercings
differing only in which side the chain hangs. And does it accompany a
tragus, industrial, helix, or orbital.

Not even a moment later could we ever possibly feel as close and as real.

Spray paint cans and open bedroom windows, graffiti like love notes.
And he sprays something about suicide across the ceiling. Small tattoos
on my fingers, your name across my wrist. The sweetest but darkest
just because you've ever seen, you'll always see,
because razors write in permanence.

Craving a journey, we turn up the voice of Sebastian Bach. Lock the
bedroom door,
leap out the window like small warriors into the night. Returning wide
awake and restless a few hours later. Still not free enough, but high
enough.

Laughing away our scratched knees, the sin and sorrows burning in the
joint passed hand to hand. Another sugar cube dissolving on the tip of
wicked tongues.
Numbing time. Holding time with bittersweetness.
Sweet she tastes, as she lowers my lips below her waist.
Wasted, thinking any place exists past this. Feeling homeless but warm
inside the pockets of her pants like still no other place has.

Reminiscing about cigarettes smoked in bathroom stalls and schoolyard brawls. We walk the halls like some group of misfits, breaking Jack Daniel's bottles in the street. Jagged, glass-like thoughts.

Lying holding hands, staring at the neon posters and black-lit walls. Your room a rainstorm, we shelter in place, inside ourselves. Close, but you feel elsewhere. They are all elsewhere,
but still alive in my porn.

Trying to understand whether it's childhood trauma or teenage rebellion keeping us together. Keeping us all here, medicated and pinned to the corners of our own self-loathing.

Then it's one pill, two pills, and stillness paired with Pink Floyd. And how I learn in one night just how to build *The Wall*.

Those pretty boys with long hair and black nail polish. Girls with shaved heads and leg hair.
We tune in, then drop out. Drift away again.

I ask you where you've been, and I've never heard of that place before. It sounds far away.

Man, we are all so far away. The stars never looked that close again, love never felt that real. How sad adolescence is, wasted on a place such as youth.

To not appreciate how high you have to be, you get to be,
before the only place to go is down.

I can't bring her back or bring us back.
Hell, I don't even know who she is anymore.

I wonder, when she remembers, if I am still her James Dean in my leather motorcycle jacket, her black silk panties bunched up in that zippered breast pocket. How we kissed for hours underneath scarred lips and black eyeliner.

We passed cigarettes and love notes through the hole in the screen and fantasized about the way we would touch each other's bodies on the other side.
If we got to the other side.

You kept saying *Are we there yet? Are we there yet?*
and I didn't have an answer. I never had the answers.

But I have those moments memorized,
I have all of you memorized.

SOMETHING ELSE BREATHING

The lungs of a Harley-Davidson,
growling of an airplane belly, glasspacks on a 4x4 pickup truck,
snowplow's rumble, screeching school bus,
popping of a lawnmower, a rusted muffler, a buzzing Weedwacker,
       anything—
the bass from the Honda a couple of doors down driven by the three-
semester senior with his high-top Adidas and the start of a curly blond
mullet,
the sound of a ringing phone,
the excruciating one-hundred-twenty-five-decibel car alarm only five
decibels below the threshold of ear pain,
an ambulance wailing,
       something—
something else out here breathing,
hanging on to life
louder
than I am.

WHEN WORDS FALL AWAY

I listen to your voice with my eyes,
and in silence
I hear your soul.

EIGHTH NOTE GROOVE

In the background
of another dark morning,
fog falls over the trees,
a thick skin stretched
over a skeleton.

Traffic in the distance stalls,
trains rumble,
leaving the echo of steel wheels
over steel rails.

Ice melts in long, steady streams,
the wind chimes battle the breeze,
a beat all its own, a new take on the standard 8th note groove,
drumming its own solo tune.

Winds here bully the naked branches,
or maybe it's those branches, always flirting with the wild air.
(Either way, I'm not one to judge.)

A spider plays dead in its web,
the *Welcome Winter* snowman flag perched from the deck ledge
quivers and wraps itself tight
around the pole,
trying not to feel any more
than it must.

GOOD INTENTIONS

My good intentions are there, they're around. You know, the ones that actually call back and aren't so argumentative all the time. The intentions that want to be tender and loving, that don't forget to say *I love you* when you leave, kiss you when you come home.

Lately, they hide so you can't see them, ducking down in ditches the minute you drive by. I know I've seen them in vacant lots, old construction sites, under two-by-fours and useless wooden pallets, in the rust growing on the once-polished metal beams cargo-ed in by freight trains and left abandoned by unemployed, underpaid contractors at work zones now deemed hazardous.

My good intentions hide lazily in overgrown fields knee-high with tall weeds, the colorful kinds that passersby mistake as wildflowers. Between you and me, you really don't even have to look that hard; I see them all the time, littered all over the landscape of your body, even sleeping inside your pillowcase or out front in the driveway, stretched out in the bed of my truck.

A time or two you've snuck up, interrupting them, which makes them defensive. Good intentions then feel no choice but to go bad, thinking they want to go back to hanging out with the rest of them, those other *good-gone-bad* ones. The ego is a powerful deterrent.

Good intentions seem to have young hearts. They mistakenly believe they are lounging out where life is, under piles and piles of objectives that are still learning to be productive, that is until you catch one. Then it's all hide-and-seek, but they were never taught the real rules of the game. They never go seeking, but they sure do like to hide. My good intentions won't tell you this, so I might as well: they really do like it when you find them, so I hope you don't stop looking.

BE HER(E) AGAIN

Gone with the turn of the ignition,
tires squealing out in the opposite direction of where home is,
or at least the place we pretended it to be.
You said you wouldn't be here again,
wouldn't start smoking again,
wouldn't start drinking again.
Said you wouldn't love or fuck up like this
again.

Another story of sex and intimacy ends with broken promises and
resentment.
When you can't stand to see them.
A time that takes touch, breaks trust
again and again.

The sound of screen doors swinging, car doors slamming.
Our last words running up and down the block.
The cold and closed sound
of good times and goodbyes.

You can say you won't, you always say you won't,
come apart over someone again.

So that they are all your pieces, and you all their pieces.
The same places and passions,
the same shared experiences and possessions.

You said you wouldn't be here again,
wouldn't be
her again.

WHO WE WISH WE WERE

In between making nothing at all,
we make calls,
make dinner,
make love.

As we learn to make sense
of these touch-and-go moments
and paint-by-number dreams.

THEY SAY IT TAKES THIRTY DAYS TO MAKE OR BREAK A HABIT

and after fifteen days, fourteen nights of silence,
I've mastered making darkness a daytime thing.
Moved the sun and moon around like curtains.
Manipulated windows into closed, locked doors.
Chandeliers into black holes in the ceiling,
candles into meaningful conversation.

PART III
Swiss Army

Show me your hands,
and I will know how you are living.

BREAKING NIGHT (URBAN SLANG TO MEAN STAYING UP UNTIL MORNING)

I'm breaking night again.
These days more gently, and graciously.
These days less tossing and turning. More up early with patience and
gratitude.
Beneath cool, light sheets,
I am acceptance.

This body knows almost nothing of regret,
of when I laid myself down like a road
for those to get on, those I got off.
How I boiled myself over like water, just to feel pure again.

Mind pounding viciously, blurred by dreams and behavior.
Where the enemy was neither in my hands nor my thoughts,
    muddying any clear view of decency.

Knows almost nothing of that sickness.

Still hard to keep those memories, even the ones that make me smile.
Mostly, the ones that look like them.

We couldn't create those now,
not from this place of peace.
My energy tamed, meeker, mild.

I'm nearly healed here, how I wish I was when you knew me.

I make you up now.
You live here contentedly
and I don't run
and I give you what you need.
Here, in this new place,
I don't leave.
And you don't leave.

WHAT'S BROKEN

The summer sky—smothered with clouds torn open to let down a little light.

The handle of this coffee mug—super-glued long ago.

Dishwasher—a do-it-yourself quick fix I must not have done right. Now I wash by hand.

Gold Figaro chain—a few links fallen out, now tighter around my neck.

Pink peony flower—too strong for its own good, now a playground for a hundred black ants.

Birdhouse—rotten and weathered.

Mailbox—not seen through the rearview mirror.

Doorbell I won't fix, now that I'm not inclined to answer the door.

Screen slider—crooked track, teaching me to make friends with the flies and spiders who have extended their outdoor living space.

Radio in my pickup truck.
Water spigot.
Some light switches—another DIY project I couldn't fix myself.

A few bones I'm sure I never noticed.
Lawn—at least once a week under a dull blade.
Her heart a time or two. Or three.

These thoughts—damaged by language and space.
Brass Zippo—old and tarnished.
Dog's collar.
And too many relationships to try to fix.

CRUSHED CARDBOARD CONTAINER

When you leave, the time I know is the last time, I buy a pack of cigarettes.
Not the kind I smoke, but the brand you do. I want to spend time back inside you, have your taste back on my lips in the same way you took me in, momentarily consumed by you. A part of our old world alive, right here.

I reminisce about the parts I shouldn't say out loud: memories around intimacy and sex, and how both should stay a bit private if you respect each other enough. The nicotine burns against the back of my throat, reminding me how we would lie afterward and smoke. After we made love, after we talked for hours on the phone.

We sure had a way of being *those kinds* of lovers—fucking like we were drunk or complete strangers, and other times knowing the other's body so well it might as well have been our own. Maybe that was just too much, most of the time.

I still don't have answers to those questions, the ones that haunted us and came up in the dark after those nights we were all thunder and storm.

If there is a right answer, that would mean one of us would be wrong, and honestly, I would rather that not be. So instead, I pretend I'm still in thought, still questioning the things around us.

I only take a couple hits, then flick the cigarette far out into the yard. I don't want to put it out; I want to watch it burn itself out all on its own.

Afterward, I'll hide the pack, knowing I'll forget where it is, and I want that.
When it's time to find you again, or when you want me to, I know I will come across this crushed cardboard container, and then I will pause, and light another.

For now, I watch the cigarette kill itself and I let myself forget.

IF YOU SEE HER

Inspired by Bob Dylan's "If You See Her, Say Hello"

you can mention I still have her baggy black sweatshirt with the hole in
the right sleeve cuff from cupping my cigarette outside her car window;
her reading glasses—looking through, seeing both sides now;
box of love letters—or just letters that, at the time, I didn't know were
coming from my heart, not my mouth;
album of pictures I still look at when I want to be taken back.
How still, her eyes and skin
shine and blind me.
While I want to remember, I hardly remember
who it is in most of these photos now—
          that smile, the smoke, the booze
isn't me anymore.
And this spring sun sure is bright, so don't go talkin' 'bout these
mirrored glasses hidin' any tears.
If you want, you can mention that of all the hundreds of books on these
shelves,
E. E. Cummings's *Erotic Poems* sees me first when I walk into the room,
that I still fondle the inscription, *You are my Poetry,*
written before I had even written most of my own.

Can mention when I said *Love always,* I still do.
Can mention I said thank you for teaching me you can love and still let
go,
and that hearing an old lover's name doesn't have to hurt.
That from time to time, in conversation, I hear she's doing well, in love,
and how that color always looked good on her.

If you do see her, just don't stare,
don't look too long.
You know what they say: women like that can steal a soul.

Just look at her a little, smile casually just long enough to pass,
and if she asks if I asked

you to say *Hello,*
say you ain't too sure.
(Doesn't have to be true.)

Say it took a minute, say I looked a little lost on her name,
say it looks like I might have forgotten it all.

And if you forget to mention most of this,
that's okay, just say *No,*
say you don't think I mentioned saying *Hello.*

LAST NIGHT AGAIN

Strength comes in getting up and getting on with it
even with a pounding headache, stabbing jolts of neuropathy,
debilitating back pain,
sweating hands, trembling,
begging for just one more . . .

Spinning, nightmares, memories,
grief, regret, shame, and spinning again.
All the spinning.

Still pulling yourself together every goddamn morning
as if that wasn't you
smashing mirrors for staring, screaming at shadows,
punching walls. Agitated, restless, vomiting,
ransacking drawers and cabinets for one more
intoxicant.

Strength comes every single day.

It's getting up and getting on with it
as if that wasn't you falling and breaking apart
last night.

BITTER FAREWELL

I'm not sorry. In my mind, I don't go easy on you.
Easy like the criminal justice system, easy like another drink,
easy like your body and her body
in places hard decisions should have been made.
Decisions that take a little bit of respect, and a whole lot of respect.

You have the audacity to reach out, invite yourself back into my life
casually, through a phone screen you knew would display your name.
As if this body in distance isn't its own communication,
you said *Don't. Speak. Please.*
then some bullshit about speaking your name.
As if you choose what injuries my body remembers.
As if you choose what I felt in battle.

I waited long to put it into words,
long for anger. Not long in life or love.
Those things are longed for, and we don't want to know when life or
love ends,
but in madness, this has taken a long fucking time.

Knowing you know me as you do, or at least knew me when I was
sitting at the bottom, piss-drunk and hungover, a smile on my face as I
walked to the counter
where a box of my favorite waited, how sweet of you, and I sweeter too
when full of Zinfandel.

I don't give a damn what you don't want me to speak.
Trust me—I wanted to unwrite you, unread you, untouch the skin
around you,
wanted to undo and unlike you,
unlove the cold surrounding you.
I wanted to unforgive, unregret, unspeak, untell, unlet you bring me
down.

To unharm me, unremember you, unlove you

for all the hurt you have done. To undrink that night,
to un-be, to unsee, to forget most of who you are.

Now it's too late for that; not even in thought can we go back to how
close I kept us.

Kept you warm under the tent beneath the stars, in the middle of the
night when it stormed, when we stayed awake laughing at the noises
the rain made; or kept you close as we walked for miles along the coast
of Mexico, beaches and mountains stretched out behind us; kept your
ring around my neck, your pictures in my wallet, kept your kiss-me-
again eyes—
kept your hair up in the emergency room when you had no clue how the
night before, when I wasn't there, you drank too much and smashed
your head on the bar floor;
how I stayed up late to pick you up the second time you were arrested
for DUI.
(Maybe you should consider getting sober too.)

Kept you too close for my own good.
And I read that text and wanted to go all *fuck you* and belligerent and
say obscene things I might mean, but knew I wouldn't mean for long.

How underneath it all, we were once children, sitting and listening to
screaming and yelling, cradling ourselves from violence, knowing most
of those words said were in anger.
It's just hurt, it's all anger
as if that gives anyone a right, gave you a right to do what you did.

Instead, I didn't respond. Not saying anything was far worse than
anything I had to say, like how at this point when I see your name, I
can't even think about the songs we used to play, or how we spent our
days riding west for miles on those motorcycles, yes, we
rode long
and we rode each other
hard.

Now I can't even say that crosses my mind, which is the worst part because man,
you should still cross my mind!

Crossed like the bandages I wore over bullet wounds, crossed like the lines you scored up on the kitchen table, crossed like the lanes you couldn't stay inside when you were too wasted to drive.
Crossed like those lines of betrayal that even a stranger, an enemy, would know better than to pass.

Can't you feel it? I have given it back.
It's all yours now.

I am not asleep inside of what you ask me not to say.
My story is not some quiet candle burning on an altar, waiting for others to pass and pray for me in sympathy.
No. I did not *give this to God.*

Your voice was once personal,
all hushed and low-toned and perverted on the other end of the phone,
always a secret inside a secret, a conversation dressed in drag.
Maybe you do repent silently to all the mystical gods that be,
but not me.

I will speak
with no empathy for the things you create
with your loud and foolish hands, dilated pill-puffed pupils,
and *Really!?* The *Will I be next* image of a child set as the picture on your profile?
How could you?
Did you already forget you held a gun in your hand?
You are who you warn against.
You are not separate from the violence of this crime-ridden, murder-capital city.

We change and time passes, I get that.
I can only hope you've grown out of the person you used to be.

I know I have, so I can only assume life's changed you too.

But you are still that careless shooter,
maybe more cowardly than criminal,
aiming at the back of the unarmed.

Baby, *sticks and stones may break our bones*, but words—you say they
hurt you?

What hurts is the selfish way
you went all trigger-crazy
and reckless,
acting like some crazed psycho
then faking tears like it was accidental.
An accident?
Guns don't shoot people; people shoot people.

So, shhh—
Don't you tell me *Don't speak.*
It may have taken a long time, but
honey, I just started talking.

SHOULD HAVE CHECKED CALLER ID

Hello?

      Hi, it's me.
      Remember me?

Yeah.

      Still think of you.
      Alone?

Yeah.

      Can I come?

No.

      Quickie?

No.

      Still with her?

Yeah.

      The bar then?

Quit drinking.

      The car, smoke up?

Quit smoking.

      Get away, I'll make it worth it.
      I know you want to.

You do?

      So, coffee then?

No.
No more.

      Who is this!?

It's me.

PERCEPTION

Desire to kneel
head down between my knees.

A transcendence of my channels surrender,
worship, sin.
Becoming
lost, found; alive, dead.
This beautiful, awful success of
God pleasure, God love, God sex, God power.

Where I'd give anything,
let you take everything,
and we spin and dance
until we crash.
Out of control, we rise like devils.
When I wanted it all,
when you gave it all my
God illusion, God perception.

ANTITHETICAL

I repent to myself often,
to you, and our "us-ness"—
when crawling across your queer body,
long and lengthy. Solid like a pew.
Not in a church, but rather my bedroom,
when I resurrect you back into my bed.
King-sized but made for two queens.
There—an offering of self, and sacrifice.
Pressed palms to your holiness,
the truest religion of all.
Anchored
rib-to-rib,
hip-to-hip.
Here we take turns being mercy
and begging for it.

IN GREEK MYTHOLOGY, ECHO IS A NYMPH WHO PROCLAIMED HER LOVE OF NARCISSUS UNTIL NOTHING WAS LEFT OF HER BUT HER VOICE

To cling too tight only hardens and strengthens my hands,
and I don't want to try that hard to be tough.
Not here, with warm eyes and flush lips.

A virginal noticing, you not known yet this way.

If it is only a moment, a brief channeling when you come, I'll let you.
Will not grab for you in the space you appear and disappear.
Loosen me. Pass through me. Teach me more about fluidity, how to flow
again like water.

Transform us, allow us to see and feel another state of being.

I am trying to translate your body into words. A place I can run away to
while trying to keep what you liked of me in reach.

Somewhere in the dark dusty corner of this room, it is still 2020, 2001,
maybe 1997. Behind a picture, behind a picture, behind a picture
in an 8 x 10 brown wooden frame. Three times my skin new since then.

I feel ghosts.
This body a wound, a warrior.
Was me, wasn't me; still the same. And we cannot remember
everything, something is always lost.

I am weak to the neck. Tiny muscles holding and choosing what's felt.
A tunnel holding all the places eyes go, tongues go,
and I wonder where you wander when you leave while kissing me.

We are these parts.
Hands touching what is desired, halting our fingers from further
exploring.

Come undone, over and under me.
With many you(s) inside me, you're easy to get used to.

Still, I am trying to translate your body into words, the latitude and
longitude of flesh.

A place inside your landscape where we press and lie pretty ourselves
as soft purple lilacs.
Where light and airy natural grasses blow.
Their fluffy seedheads, slender, attractive stems practically dancing in
the breeze of this Windy City.

And below in the long, dark grooves, in the depths of forged cornfields,
my voice echoes back.
Returns—taking the shape of you.

BLACK CROW & GRAVEL ROADS

It was one of those roads, situated usually between fields and acres, a loose surface with washouts, corrugations, and road dust. A road driven for a mindful experience not found on the interstates and highways, traffic and tollways. They say roads should be blacktopped when they exceed five hundred cars a day, but there isn't enough revenue in Illinois even to maintain the roads they've made, let alone pave all the old ones, and I am happy about that.

The gravel teaches us life isn't smooth; it's just as bumpy for us as it is for the next, teaches us to slow down, sometimes to pull over to let others pass, and to keep our mouths shut. Those ups and downs can rattle teeth at times, and there's a bigger lesson there too.

When I saw the black crows all hovering near the side of the road, I pulled over. I thought maybe I would save some poor animal, its moral dignity, by tucking it under the tall grass, away from the eyes that would stare at its body as they passed, but when I got out of my car, all I could hear was the loud *CAW CAW CAW*, and those big black birds didn't move. They took turns flaring their chests and wings, visiting the ground and circling. I walked closer into the cawing and saw a mangled, headless crow, its blood staining the gravel. I realized they were in mourning, cawing as if it were a memorial, a funeral right there on the road.

I stood by, then stood down, so they could weep for their friend in peace.

WE SANG ALONG IN REBELLION AND MADE OUT IN THE NAME OF SELF-EXPRESSION

Those '90s Midwest summer nights,
raw-boned, burnt out,
suicide drinks and Southern Comfort, long drags, one-hitters,
more alive hour to hour within that kiss of someone else's body.

A coming together of headbanger and flower child,
leather jackets, sleeveless flannels, Metallica and Megadeth T-shirts,
combat boots and hemp-woven sandals,
patchouli and vanilla,
reading Bukowski and Vonnegut,
Ginsberg and Kerouac,
singing classic songs by Joplin, Steve Miller, Dylan, and Joni Mitchell,
and we sing, as she sings, about clouds, and love, and the illusions of it
all.

Later, I'm ransacking my memory for those feelings
balled up somewhere in coiled bedsheets, dirty laundry
keeps on, keeps on
going missing,
just loose change, another penny for my thoughts.

We roll
another rolling stone, in and out, habit after habit,
hanging out car windows,
primer-painted Chevy Novas and El Caminos.

We wait at the corner of Mallard Lake Forest Preserve, and then he rolls
up with her,
both with their feathered David Cassidy hair.
We get in, and soon, in the front seat,
he's kissing him as she's stretched out in the back,
Doc Martens, ripped fishnets, ringed fingers, bitten nails, smeared
black makeup,

some poster child for destruction and rusted, bloodstained razors.
The radio asks about moving on from here, and along with the chorus,
we sing about blue jeans and baby queens.
I look over at you when David Essex mentions
the prettiest girl he has ever seen.

And the smoke hazes through the rearview
as we look mirror to mirror,
asking to lose ourselves
when really, creating a place to belong.

Folded in those back seats, piled elbow to elbow,
she and her close to second base,
just an unsnapped bra away,
him in his Levi's 501s just a couple buttons down from blown,
and in those Midwest summers with their suede rawhide moons,
we sure thought we knew something
about life, about love,
convinced this was where we had
learned it all.

REFLECTION

It's difficult to do, telling you of this love,
though I fully remember everything.

Sit awhile with me beneath this cottonwood.
We can gain great insight into a tree by looking hard and still at its leaf.

A much smaller, simpler piece of what once was.

BURNING BRIDGES, BURNING SAGE

It does not come to stay, comes to pass
like time, always on the move.
Does not stop when it feels something, even when something might be love.

Tonight, I don't stop.

I'm diaphragm-breathing, slowly, taking you in about ten breaths per
minute.
Watching the owl, wiser by her night haunts,
teaches me to see the enemy because of the dark,
not despite.
My dreams say what they mean, they just don't use day language.
The night is audible enough.

Revealing how love opens our eyes, then blinds us.
Leaves an open chest cavity, a wound to grope
the dark.
Trying to feel the presence of *tangible*, anything
close enough to grab.
Our feelings we dare not say out loud, even when we want to. Even when
we wish our lover to read our minds. (Especially then.)

When I think of our nakedness, I don't burn red candles,
the traditional color of love, of hearts.
Seducing the places between our legs;
we, silent.

Instead, I burn sage,
then invite all the gods and goddesses
hitchhiking with their thumbs out
to land here in the powerful magic of the dark.

Instead, I burn bridges,
knowing it does not matter who those we love are now;
it only matters how we remember them when we breathe them in.

Right now, you're coming in about twelve breaths per minute.

I'm working through my past, knowing no one is innocent. Not even
Spring.
She openly buries all her lovers and ghosts
then starts over again every year.

Like her, I have lifetimes in a single cycle of season, curling into my
animus.
Holding masculinity as close as any other sensitive feeling
that declares its need to stand up strong.

I am not decorated entirely of that body, nor gentle materials either.
Like these pink petals pressed against a scented rose,
the feminine feeling of the flesh.

I am multitudes, coming out in torrents
even when you ask politely
for a light, soft rain.

Instead, between breaths,
my downpour floods this black shingled roof.
Here my heat is humid steam rising,
a white fog dancing its way to suicide.

Often there is a teeter, then a fall, an unfolding when I am at my best.
A wanting to please you in ways different than what I say please for.

You said my skin was softer than it looked. Closing my eyes,
I run my finger along the inside of my forearm,
knowing the body is not separate from what it keeps inside.

A wildness running beneath this skin line,
and years, months, days, moments
like us, like time

coming to pass.

GONE NOW

Once, I kneeled
to pray to your venom, like vodka, like violence;
your breath, like love, like lies, like loneliness,
like lost—
that doesn't ask but shows up like dreams, like devils,
that touches like woman, like worship,
like wreckage.

I didn't walk away,
gave like boi, like body, like betrayal
underneath the holding of child, making better the battles
like surrender, like seduction,
like sober.

I gave to your mercy
like memories, like monsters, like marriage.
One more chance to believe your words—like forever, like forgiveness,
like flowers—
that don't care back but take time,
like this, like tomorrow, like today,
like therapy
for the next several years

that takes me back to a past of abuse, like abandonment, like alone.
A time when I was all anger,
like alcohol, like cutting,
like crying.

Then we hold like it's better, we're better,
like we are beyond that now.
Until another episode of hate, like hurt,
like hitting.
Screaming like strangers, then sorry,
like save me,

like save me.

Your apology is like repentance, like rage, like reckless again.
Cocaine, like casualty, like chaos,
like crazy.

Then no warning, just damage.
Your gun, a guilt, like sorry has a sickness, like nightmares.
Never again, like gone now, like gone.

GHOST

The same places you haunt, I ghost.

PART IV
BUTTERFLY

She is a window, the world left open.

JANUARY TWENTY-NINTH

I'm empty of words.
The date now just another square on a January calendar.

A couple of numbers at the end of another month.
A fridge-hung reminder, a to-do list of what I should do but likely won't.
(At least not today.)

Every year more and more about you leaves me.
I've learned to let loose the feelings about you I couldn't stomach.

The details that for so long made my skin crawl and kept me sick.
The sound of your voice, the thought of ever having loved you like I did.
And then the pills, the many colorful painkillers.

Numb with rage for years.
Stuck inside all that *crazy*
and how it was just like you to like me better that way. Out of my mind,
out of control.
Vicious cycles of harming and healing.
The kind of *out of control* that had no choice but to turn itself into
madness.

On today's date, this year, this time,
finally, I have come to think of you lightly.

I remember you in all those ways from before I taught myself to hate
you.

It's peaceful in this place, a new kind of winter.
Just an ordinary, cold, quiet kind of January.

ADMIT, WE COULD GO ON LIKE THIS FOREVER

Hold me with arms
that don't ask me to be
what you need.

IN THE RAIN

In the rain, I don't dance. Don't gently drift or sway, bellowing the
words to some blues classic.
I don't look up with an open mouth, asking to taste what wet and warm
feels like.

In the rain, I feel all those sweaty palms roaming my body, slick skin
pressed to softness.
The easy flow of feeling in and out of love.

In the rain, I am all of them.
Her ex-lovers, his ex-lovers, my ex-lovers.
Touching, tracing, and tingling their way down, the way only something
falling
can.

WARMER SEASONS

We linger, cigarette smoke on cold windows,
a kiss so deep, a memory of warmer seasons.
We linger a heartbeat intense enough to rattle the silence.
A promise this body can keep.

I distort the lines of poetry and confession.

Lying here, staring long into the walls. My sober mind leading me into
hallucinations.
I watch pink roses grow across '70s wallpaper.
Even after a good sleep, a hard rain, and the morning sunshine, the
flowers can still smell sad.

I am not ready to move or love just yet.
I am here, holding something about us together, though so much has
already fallen apart we should be giving it away.
Still, I long to press myself firmly against the breast of your tight black
T-shirt, push my heart into your heart, into your ghost.

To her, I give so easily the one thing you wanted of me.
A kiss so deep, a memory of warmer seasons.

HOPE

I am falling into memory
and all that is still alive
inside its arms.

I CANNOT THROW LOVE OUT THE WINDOW

*Written in response to one of Rimbaud's lines from Complete Works,
Selected Letters*

Yes, Arthur Rimbaud, you can
turn love into something small, press it, smash it, make it into a ball
and toss it out the window onto the highway at sixty miles per hour,
just not in traffic,
not in front of a cop.

Throw it down onto the floorboard, step on it, stomp it, kick it, break it,
then throw it as hard as you can towards the west as the sun sets, along
the back road on your way home.
Or save it, carry it into your house,
spread love out
across the living room floor, light the corners with a lighter, watch it
burn.

Laugh at it, spit on it, soak it in vinegar and drop it from the second-
story window.
Write love right out of your body.
Sweat it out.
Cut it out.
Put your finger down your throat and gag love out into the toilet,
then flush—

LESSONS FROM THE WEATHER

The meteorologist for Channel 9 WGN said
*It will only take seventeen and a half minutes in today's sun to burn your
skin.*
I thought how you must be taking lessons from the weather.
A few minutes here, a couple there,
then shade the sunburn.

The way you've become as good as:
Can't right now, now's not a good time, don't call me, I'll call you.
From the start, you settled for second.

I know I'm shallow for liking the Karma
though I know it's only half true.

The real answers are in the questions we choose not to ask.
I, too, don't care to ask.

Instead, I flip the channel and stay inside.
Wait for the weather to get its shit together.

PORCH LIGHTS

There is something that says *I love you*
in porch lights left on
after dark.

THE POEM THAT FINDS YOU IN THE MIDDLE OF MOVING ON

I smile when you say *I love this one.* Makes me wonder how it is it came to you, how it found you. Was it standing outside in the cold, all wet and lonely at your doorstep with no raincoat, looking sad and hopeless—all gentle and helpless?

Was it waiting at a traffic-control device while you were stuck at a red light? Standing in the roadway, banging with closed fists on your driver's-side window? Afraid the glass would shatter, afraid it might cause a scene, did you say, *Okay, I'll listen, I'll read this one, but I only have a minute, then I must go*?

Maybe it found you in your recliner at 8 p.m., the evening yours alone, the way sometimes I still wish I was. Lying back, reading the poem, just another story of my soul, while nourishing yours, nursing whiskey.

If I am lucky, maybe it snuck up from behind, wrapped its warm hands around you. Holding you one morning as you stood at the counter in front of the French press, just out of the shower. A towel bunched around your breast. Closing your eyes momentarily, the voice a welcoming, a remembering of something missing.

I guess I'll never know where you were or what you were doing when you let those words speak to you. It's probably best I don't.

I smile, content in knowing every now and then, I still know how to find you.

HAPPINESS IS

Happiness is interstates and winding pavements, back roads, and
shortcuts,
her sunglasses on my dashboard.
It's early morning sunrises that don't need to take your breath away,
they just exist and ask you to notice.
It's starry nights and half-moons, full moons on chilly nights,
fires, flames, warm skin, and sunburns.
It's feeling small in a big world and feeling large in our own life.
It's the way coffee tastes first thing in the morning and those sugar-
cream smiles that say I'll see you again, later.
It's letters in lunch boxes, on steamed bathroom mirrors, writing my
name on your skin with my fingertips across your body in the dark.
It's the smell of your hair—a world I want to breathe in.
It's puppies that become dogs that become companions that become
our best friends.
It's painting white walls in color to make this place feel more like home.
It's growing vegetables to feed our souls, raising something, even a
plant, together.
It's thumbtacks on maps that say we have been here, and a list of places
we're still eager to see.
It's long walks at sunrise, and sunset, watching monarchs.
It's waiting up.
It's falling asleep in back seats, airplanes, on the couch to your favorite
movie.
It's reading out loud when you want to hear my voice.

Happiness is thinking about you and smiling even if together we often
hurt.
It's songs that speak to the child in us, an understanding of how far
we've come.
It's coming this far with a desire to keep going.
It's folded pages in notebooks because you like *this* one
(that I'll keep folded because it means something to you).
It's those stories I ask you to tell me again and again.

It's the hope that's still there in your voice.
It's Dylan, Reznor, Janis, and Stevie during those afternoons I ask to feel something.
It's holding your hand, my fingers in your belt loop.
It's Tuesday—ordinary and plain.
It's doing laundry, sweeping floors, taking pride in this place we've made a home.
It's leftovers made the night before (because you know what I like).
It's old photo albums and handwritten love notes,
those secret stares and words we use that nobody else knows.
It's saying you'll be there and I know you mean it,
even if I never ask.

Happiness is creating and making something you'll remember me for.
It's making love, making mistakes, and making it up to you.
It's *good morning* on the screen when schedules do their best to keep us apart.
It's built-in bookshelves with psychology, philosophy, and poetry,
hot showers, baseball caps, high-tops, and ripped blue jeans.
It's a room full of people, but you only see me,
and the way my heart has loved you ever since.

Happiness is chrome-plated, Vance & Hines,
chasing the sun, feeling high through the wind on open highways.
It's no place to be and no place I'd rather be.
It's bandannas and cowboy hats, combat boots and Converse, leather saddles and custom tattoos.
It's opening up to that person you spent hours on the phone talking to.
It's in someone's arms where you feel a true belonging.

Happiness is creating a life worth living.
It's making art and sharing,
even if no one *gets* it,
even when no one is looking.

FORTY-TWO MILES AWAY

Out front of Salvatores Funeral Home, the marble lion sits upon its
stone throne, bold and proud,
one front paw pushing back the world, the second a cracked and broken
wound severed at the nail line.
A green Community Disposal dumpster, the oldest and cleanest in the
alley, also sits. A place where rats gather and pray not to be hunted
while scavenging what little crumbs or bone is left.

In this small town, one streetlight blinks for the living, though after
ten the streets are mostly dead. The oak- and maple-lined block glows
faintly under the soft light of porch lamps casting long-armed shadows
in the darkness. The weather of early October is coming in fast, the
branches pushing their leaves out into the world. They drift in the cool
night air. I listen, I hear—

I've carried you and held you long enough.
It's over now; you're grown.
Go now! You must go.

And through this worn-out, dirty windshield, the stars are dim
headlights in the sky. The moon and the night ride with me like old
friends who know how to keep good, quiet company.

ACTUALLY, A LOVE POEM

Lately, lifting and embracing the iron is not soothing my soul
against the hard nakedness of truth, a weeping, rare testament to the
depth and intensity
of what weighs on my mind.

Did I speak of the thorn birds yet, their fearlessness and bravery?

More importantly, how deeply they love with their little bodies,
their whole body.
Their eagerness to be pained for love speaks to the capacity of what we
have yet to give—
what a passionate burden.

I want to be taken by the force of slow conversations,
ones that whisper below the surface of our thin breath,
an actual, true surrender to language.

Words often have a mind of their own, an engendered personal agenda
teaching us to tolerate the pain of what keeps us full of passion.

I have been human a long time now. I have already been bent to the
point of invincibility,
my heart damn near unbreakable. You won't even know it's there.

If quiet,
tonight, may I still call you lover?

So many restrictions blur the sight of what is, but believe, I am still
fearless in the face of life, breathing it in every day. I think you already
hear me walking beside you.
With a voice like this, I hide no bruises.

Barefoot on this familiar ground, the only path home,
passing places of my past (tempting or saddening, I cannot tell),

likely just
another memory of my many old haunts, I suppose.

We can love and still let go, I say.
I will hold your hand and lead if you let me.

As we pass through our garden, and the flowers
watch their gentle, soft-colored petals fall,
here, we do nothing
but miss and remember the fragrance.

WHAT TO SAY TO THE THEY SITTING ON THE CURB IN FRONT OF BARNES AND NOBLE

You, in the heat of June,
wearing a black motorcycle jacket with iron-on band patches,
probably drinking flat beer in that travel mug covered with rainbow
stickers and an upside-down pink triangle,
legs stretched out over the curb
so everyone can see your black fishnets through the homemade holes
in the knees of your jeans, your punk leather zippered combat boots
tapping to the music of your headset.

You, dressed black on black with your stoner sunglasses, blowing
cigarette smoke onto everyone who passes,
laughing with whomever you're speaking to on the phone like everyone
should hear your conversation, with all your
*Like tell me about it*s and *as if*s,
like you and your friends are the first to be revolted by the culture of
this society.

Well, let me tell you *thems* something:
it's these people who pass, who you think all old and cut-out looking,
who helped pave the path for you
to show up expressed however it is
you please.

> (*I mean, I don't really say any of this—*
> *what I say is nothing.*)

I simply smile, or better yet lift my chin up,
one of those *Hey, what's up* gestures we used to do when we spotted one
of our own kind,
because *like I get it*;
there was a time when I was as punk as you,
revolted and revered, outcast,
sitting there with my *Metal Mania*, *Inked*, or *Guitar World* magazine

when that was the only literature of value.

When I was sitting on the curb, drinking flat beer, talking to someone I
was certain would be the only one that ever understood me.
Watching families and bland-looking people walk by, all dressed pretty
much the same,
thinking *I'll never be like that,*
like them,
like they are.

THE FEELINGS BETWEEN US CHANGED COLOR

and this moment here feels red, a dull red, romantic merlot, masculine
and strong but does not shout,
then blue—how thoughtful the color blue is. Such mystery sleeps inside
deep indigo.

Perhaps something calmer, safer, more classical and neutral:
ivory, a color that teaches us to see more doing less, to sit, not chase.
A coastal-colored experience, one we want to fill our palms with
to watch the tan sand crystals glitter and sparkle with wonder.

Or rather, the burnt tones of worn leather and wood,
inviting, grounding, and reliable,
the way wood continues living and breathing, responds to its
surroundings
even after it's been cut, manipulated, or beat into design,
transforming still, even after its death,
expanding and contracting over time,
shifting color
the way temperature affects mood, how with exposure to air and
sunlight, we grow.

These variations, much like those moments,
dramatic and life-changing,
painful,
and still so colorful and beautiful.

BIRD HOURS

I keep bird hours and too am desirous of watching,
but again, I mistake a mourning dove for a pigeon,
their song for heartbreak,
pause for capture,
open space for payment, a mortgage I'll never afford to pay in full.
Mistake freedom for responsibility—teaching myself not to react,
to unlearn decades of doing and doing now.

Mistake memory for your name, or lust,
or at least something that shows up looking a lot like, or nothing like,
you.

This morning, last-night thoughts pound
against my mind's walls;
forgive me for beginning our time together again with goodbye.
The covered clouds that cool have gone.
Sun now blasts through.
I see the beauty and misery,
heat and weakness,
the rise, the fall,
the art in it all.

IS-NESS OF THINGS

Unashamed of being naked, huddled under a blanket, watching old movies at midnight. Your arms unfold, revealing new, unnippled breasts, unembarrassed for me to love the hurt right out of them. Now. Here. Familiar, new strangers.
There is still so much to learn.

Remembering the leaves in the fall, how they blow and scatter and cover what's underneath: a long and rolling road still winding.
Wanting to be like that, practiced in the wonders and the mystery of our bodies, where love does not hide but twists and turns, undresses into something more comfortable,
a graceful, elegant hum, the experience sweetly unbearable.

A longing so deep I dare it not to end.

It is not wisdom that took down the walls I hurdled; it was when they fell I embraced the crumble. Knowing what I bring to the table, I never mind eating alone.

For now, the hummingbirds are pounding against the window. In their flutter, a quick decision to bolt. I must turn over my ways for softness now. Stand for something fragile.

When within the law, one is wise to fear it. In the time we spent living together, it owned a part of me, and I admit, I am afraid to give that much of myself again.

I hope it is not time alone that keeps you, but the beauty of wanting what takes time to love.
And what terrible beauty.

I am opening a door, a part of me for you to meet and warmly embrace. What is here, I ask you to boldly hold. The offer is not given to most, and I cannot bear to see you turn away.

Yesterday, a slow, controlled wind whispered to these trees, and I
thought how this was the sound of loneliness, a sensuous loneliness, a
happy yet heartbreaking symphony. You may have thought so too.

I am not shy when my heart is showing, electric and released.
I am already inside you, reaching to touch the outlines of your being.

Closed flower, it is only a wanting so dangerous in its full abandon
that can cause our petals to open.

BLACKBERRY BRANDY

When I believed I could write,
I had a liking for sweet and strong. A little hard but not too heavy.
A taste for foraged fruit and a long afterburn.
Stayed up until the early hours of the morning, slept with a lot of girls.

Those wild nights brought my reckless friends.
The right words came too. All of it
as easy as I was.

Now, life's simpler, my taste buds a bit weaker,
  and those feelings,
    the right words,
      and all the poems—
well, they don't come around
quite as often as they used to either.

FORWARD MY MAIL TO MARS

After a line from Stanley Kunitz's "The Flight of Apollo"

That's what Stanley Kunitz once said.
I say don't forward mine at all. Leave it there to disintegrate,
let it wear itself down
back to nature,
those letters, this mail.
Back to paper, to tree.
Pile it up next to the front doorstep.
Toss it in the garbage can,
the recycle bin.
Rubber-band it and give it back to the postman.
Read it.
(*You know you will.*)
Soak it in charcoal fluid,
start a fire with it,
roast marshmallows over it,
watch it burn.
Do whatever you want,
but I'd rather you not reach out.
Don't forward my mail to Mars.
Don't think of me at all.

AND NOT LOOK BACK

Can we go back?
Not the whole way, maybe half. When there was still something left to
save.

Save ourselves from "us" happening.
Before we allowed our names to mean wounds.
Before we held hands in Country Trail Pub's parking lot.
Before I crawled into the back seat of your Chevy,
before I took you home, made my place "ours,"
before we kissed drunk and got naked.
Your body a place I lived in, mine a place you only visited on nights that
turned to mornings when you couldn't be alone. I didn't want you to be
alone.

Before we claimed '90s love ballads, made promises to turn into each
other's everything.
A stake that has no choice but to fail.

Before we let love make decisions while taking away our independence.
Before I became another lover who treated you poorly; you, another
woman who couldn't love me.

Before we followed each other and looked for lies,
looked through phones and glove compartments, pants pockets and
email attachments,
looked at bodies for signs of evidence.
It's true: anyone can fit into the disguise of dishonest if we look hard
enough.
All of this to make leaving easy when all along, we were already leaving.

Before the pictures got ripped up and letters got burned,
before we both said *I don't even know you anymore.*
And we meant it, in between the times when we didn't.

Can we go back to the fairy tales in each other's eyes? The bellies full of butterflies?
When I couldn't hold you close enough and all you wanted was my touch.

Before there was testimony and statements, accusations and confessions,
before trial and sentencing, orders of protections and prison,
before intent and injury, hurt and recovery.

Before we really even knew each other.
Can we go back to that parking lot?
Keep our eyes to ourselves, unlock hands, and walk separately in our own direction?
Pull out and never, ever once look back.

What do you say, can we?

POCKET KNIVES

I hear butterfly,
I think spring action, switch activated,
think dagger, switchblade stiletto.

I think pocket knives.

I think prohibited, and unlawful use of weapons,
think steel blades and brass knuckles.
I think self-defense, Swiss Army, tactical.
I think practice.

I hear butterfly, I think combat.
Sparring battles and opponents,
physical skill and mental mindset.
I think triangulation and forty-five-degree angles,
I think grappling, shoulder width, and belt level,
think close encounters.

I hear butterfly, I think dangerous,
weak side stance and cool steel survival.

I think immense speed, think weapon.
I hear butterfly,
I think knives, I think protection.

WILD WORDS

I prefer to write in solitude, where loneliness comes closer than any
lover has.

Surrounded by words, these little wild animals
I chase across the page.
They bark, squeal, howl,
sneak, and crawl.
Stealing whatever they can wrap their paws around.
In this place, we banter and stalk each other.

I keep them fed. I keep them wild.
They keep me company.

ON WRITERS

Writers are all at once everything.

The craftsman, architect, blackbird, worm, prostitute, priest. The incarcerated and the free.

Full of tenderness, forlornness, and intimacy.
Moved by desire and lust.

And, at the same time, writers are none of those things.

As writers and artists, we can create for days, weeks, months, even years straight. Then it happens when nothing comes at all. I think about those times. What was I doing that kept me from creating? Well, I was simply *being*.

I was living, loving, and experiencing. I was making memories and mistakes and still making progress. I may not have been writing much then, but I was living in ways I'm still writing about now. It will come back; it always comes back.

Keep Growing. Keep Creating
JJ

J.J. Celli is a queer writer from the Chicago area, where she is active in the spoken word poetry scene. Celli spent over two decades fighting crime and working as a major crimes/homicide detective, later retiring as a Sergeant. As a survivor of intimate partner gun violence, she is passionate and dedicated to educating others on domestic violence in same-sex relationships, while also advocating for the LGBTQ+ community. *Love Letters and Pocket Knives* is her first collection.